PANDAS

Please visit our web site at: www.garethstevens.com
For a free color catalog describing Gareth Stevens Publishing's
list of high-quality books and multimedia programs, call
1-800-542-2595 (USA) or 1-800-387-3178 (Canada).
Gareth Stevens Publishing's fax: (414) 332-3567.

Library of Congress Cataloging-in-Publication Data available upon
request from publisher. Fax (414) 336-0157 for the attention of the
Publishing Records Department.

ISBN 0-8368-4121-2

This edition first published in 2004 by
Gareth Stevens Publishing
A World Almanac Education Group Company
330 West Olive Street, Suite 100
Milwaukee, Wisconsin 53212 USA

This U.S. edition copyright © 2004 by Gareth Stevens, Inc. Original edition
copyright © 2001 by DeAgostini UK Limited. First published in 2001 as
My Animal Kingdom: All About Pandas by DeAgostini UK Ltd., Griffin House,
161 Hammersmith Road, London W6 8SD, England. Additional end matter
copyright © 2004 by Gareth Stevens, Inc.

Editorial and design: Tucker Slingsby Ltd., London
Gareth Stevens series editor: Catherine Gardner
Gareth Stevens art direction: Tammy Gruenewald

Picture Credits
Bruce Coleman Collection — John Cancalosi: cover and title page; Hans Reinhard:
    12 (top), 29; Gerald S. Cubbit: 14-15; Sophy and Michael Day: 15 (top); Erwin
    and Peggy Bauer: 19 (top), 26.
Pictor International: 14, 23, 28.
Harry Smith Collection: 20.
Tony Stone Images — Tim Davies: 8, 9 (left), 11; Keren Su: 9 (right), 11 (inset),
    12 (bottom), 13, 17, 18, 19 (bottom); Daniel J. Cox: 16, 24 (inset); Rosemary
    Calvert: 21; Pal Hermansen: 24-25; Peter Pearson: 27.

Printed in the United States of America

1 2 3 4 5 6 7 8 9 08 07 06 05 04

PANDAS

Gareth Stevens Publishing
A WORLD ALMANAC EDUCATION GROUP COMPANY

PANDA FACTS

ANIMAL GROUP: mammal

COLOR: black and white

SIZE: 4 to 5 feet (1.2 to 1.5 meters) long. Males can measure up to 3 feet (1 m) from foot to shoulder. Females are usually a little smaller.

WEIGHT: 190 to 265 pounds (85 to 120 kilograms)

SPEED: Pandas walk very slowly, rarely even breaking into a jog.

EATS: bamboo shoots, stalks, and leaves; flowers; and small animals

DRINKS: lots of water. Pandas make sure they are never far from a good supply of water.

LIVES: up to 25 years

CONTENTS

Words that appear in the glossary are printed in
boldface type the first time they occur in the text.

A Closer Look

Giant pandas are large animals, but they are not really as big as giants. They are called giant pandas because they are so much bigger than red pandas. Giant pandas and red pandas are related, but giant pandas look like bears, and red pandas look more like **raccoons**.

Giant pandas have distinctive black and white coats, yet they are hard to see in the wild. Pandas are very shy around people, and their coats blend in with the snowy forests in which they live. With possibly fewer than one thousand pandas left in the world, they are also very rare.

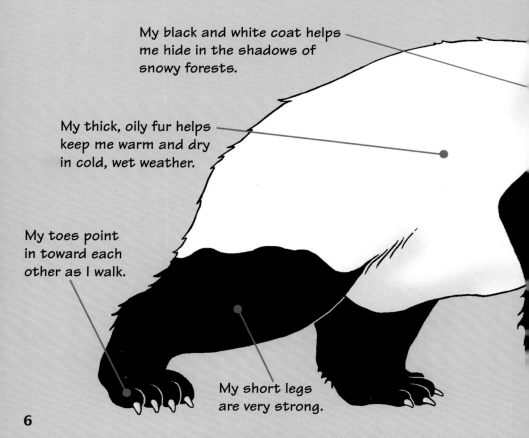

My black and white coat helps me hide in the shadows of snowy forests.

My thick, oily fur helps keep me warm and dry in cold, wet weather.

My toes point in toward each other as I walk.

My short legs are very strong.

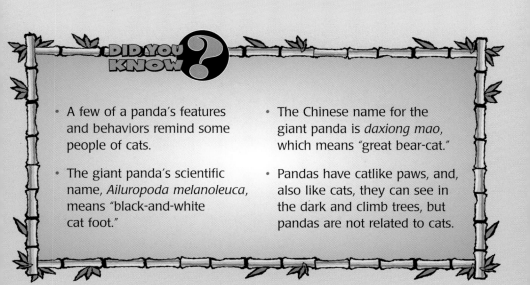

- A few of a panda's features and behaviors remind some people of cats.

- The giant panda's scientific name, *Ailuropoda melanoleuca*, means "black-and-white cat foot."

- The Chinese name for the giant panda is *daxiong mao*, which means "great bear-cat."

- Pandas have catlike paws, and, also like cats, they can see in the dark and climb trees, but pandas are not related to cats.

I have sharp hearing, so I can easily sense danger.

My eyes let in extra light when I need it, so I can see well in the dark.

I have a sensitive nose, so I can sniff out the scents left by other pandas.

My teeth are very strong, so I can chew through tough bamboo.

To survive in the wild, a giant panda depends on its teeth and its toes. Giant pandas have big, strong teeth with wide, flat **molars** that are perfect for crushing hard bamboo stalks. Bamboo, which is the giant panda's main food, is a very tough plant. Even using both hands, a strong person cannot break a thick piece of fresh bamboo. A panda can snap the same piece of bamboo in two with just one bite! A giant panda needs its sharp claws to tear off and hold bamboo shoots, to climb trees when it needs to escape from danger, and to defend itself when an enemy attacks.

PERFECT PAWS

sharp claws for tearing, gripping, and climbing

thick pad to protect bottom of foot

false thumb

A panda has unusual paws, but they are perfect for holding bamboo and the other plants pandas eat. On each of its front paws, a panda has an extra **digit** known as "the panda's thumb." It is not like a human thumb. It is actually a long wrist bone covered with a pad of skin. A panda uses its false thumb the same way people use their thumbs. It helps the panda get a good grip on an object.

CLIMBING BEARS

Pandas love to climb trees. With their special paws and long claws, they can climb high to escape from danger or from any unwanted visitors. Going up is easy, but climbing down can be tricky. When they are just a short distance from the ground, pandas will often jump down — and land with a thump!

HOME, SWEET HOME

Giant pandas are an endangered **species**, which means that few of them remain in the wild, and they are in great danger of dying out completely. Some giant pandas live in zoos throughout the world, but those still in the wild can be found only in a small part of China. They live in bamboo forests in the mountains. The forests are cold, wet, and, in winter, snowy. Bamboo forests are very thick, with lots of trees and other plants — and plenty of hiding places.

WHERE IN THE WORLD?

Giant pandas live in southwestern China, in the Sichuan Province and a few neighboring provinces. They stay close to the bamboo forests, which supply most of their food. Giant pandas make their homes in mountain ranges and roam at **altitudes** between about 3,600 and 11,000 feet (1,100 and 3,300 meters). If bamboo is growing higher on a mountain, giant pandas will climb higher to reach it. They have been known to climb to altitudes as high as 13,000 feet (4,000 m).

- Adult pandas spend most of their time alone.

- Each panda has a **territory** that covers up to 4 square miles (10 square kilometers). One panda's territory might overlap another's, but both of the pandas will try to avoid each other.

- Giant pandas try to stay away from all other animals, especially humans.

- Because pandas live alone and are not often seen, the Chinese used to call them "the **hermits** of the forest."

HIDE AND SEEK

During cold, snowy months, a panda's patchy black-and-white coat is an excellent **camouflage**. The colors and patterns blend into wintry shadows perfectly.

NEIGHBORS

Giant pandas are very shy and stay away from all animals, including each other. To avoid meeting other pandas, each giant panda marks its territory with a scent. The panda rubs its bottom against trees and rocks, leaving behind a sticky, smelly liquid. The smell lets other pandas know that a giant panda is already using that area of land. The smell also tells whether the panda is a male or a female. When a giant panda smells another panda's scent, it will go away — and stay away!

BRIGHT BIRDS

Golden pheasants are beautiful birds that share the bamboo forests with giant pandas. The male bird uses his bright coloring to attract female birds, which have plainer colors.

NOSY NEIGHBOR

A panda sitting in a tree might just find itself next to the unusual-looking golden snub-nosed monkey.

FOREST FRIEND

Another animal a giant panda might meet in the forest is a pika. The pika is a **mammal** that is a lot like a rabbit, but smaller. Unlike pandas, pikas usually live in groups. Like pandas, pikas cannot run very well. Instead of running, a pika moves in little jumps.

FISHING CAT

Although most cats do not like water, the clever fishing cat lives near water and can swim very well. This cat's toes are partially webbed to help it catch the small water animals it likes to eat. The fishing cat usually scoops fish out of the water with its paws, but, at times, it even dives into the water after them.

OTHER BAMBOO-EATERS

RED PANDA

The raccoonlike red panda might not look much like its "giant" cousin, but it, too, eats bamboo.

BAMBOO RAT

Like a giant panda, a bamboo rat has big, strong teeth to help it chew tough stalks of fresh bamboo.

TAKIN

A takin looks like an ox, but it is about the same size as a giant panda, and it likes bamboo as much as a panda does.

THE FAMILY

Giant pandas do not live in groups — they live alone. Even young pandas leave their mothers when they are about eighteen months old, and once they leave, they live alone. When pandas meet by chance in the wild, they either ignore each other or fight to decide whose territory they are on.

Adult pandas come together for a few days each spring to look for mates. They use their sensitive noses and many different barking and whining sounds to find each other. At this time of year, pandas can be very noisy animals. During the rest of the year, giant pandas are much quieter.

Panda mothers choose safe spots, such as caves or hollow trees, to give birth to their babies. A baby panda is called a cub. Newborn panda cubs are very small, so **predators** can easily attack them. A mother panda stays with her cub, at first, but soon has to go look for food. To keep the cub safe, she carries it with her. The panda mother carries her baby by holding it gently in her mouth. At other times, she cradles it in her huge paws. When the cub cries for attention, the mother panda must try to quiet it right away. Any sound might attract enemies such as leopards or humans.

LAZING AROUND

Like all baby animals, a panda cub has a lot to learn. It cannot eat bamboo when it is young so, while its mother feeds, the cub passes the time by playing and learning. If it cannot find a tree to climb, it will often try climbing on its mother's back. Panda cubs also like to slide in the snow and, sometimes, even persuade their mothers to join in.

Baby File

Birth

Most often, giant pandas give birth to one cub at a time. A newborn cub is tiny, helpless, and almost hairless. At birth, a panda cub is about 5 inches (12 centimeters) long, and it weighs only about 5 ounces (140 grams). Its mother looks after the cub carefully and feeds it milk from her body. Soon, the cub's fur starts to grow, it opens its eyes, and it begins to crawl.

Six Months to One Year

Although, at six months old, it is able to start eating bamboo, a panda cub still drinks its mother's milk until it is about one year old. After passing its first birthday, a panda cub can take care of itself.

One-and-a-Half Years and Older

A panda cub leaves its mother at about eighteen months old, but it is not fully grown until sometime between the ages of four and seven. After a panda cub leaves its mother, it lives alone.

Favorite Foods

Giant pandas spend up to fourteen hours a day eating. Their favorite food is bamboo, which is easy to find but hard to **digest**. A giant panda has to eat a lot of bamboo to get the **nutrients** it needs to stay healthy.

Today, giant pandas mainly eat plants, but long ago, their ancestors were carnivorous, which means they ate only meat. Over time, the panda's diet has changed. Although giant pandas now eat plants most often, they sometimes will try to catch fish, pikas, or rats for food.

Munching Machine

A giant panda normally eats sitting down and, usually, surrounded by bamboo plants. The panda reaches out and bites off a stalk of bamboo. Then it strips away the tough outside covering of the stalk and quickly chews up the rest.

BEST BAMBOO

Bamboo is a plant. It is a type of woody grass that can grow as tall as a tree. Approximately twelve hundred different kinds of bamboo grow in places all over the world. Pandas eat only about twenty different kinds. In the wild, their two favorite kinds of bamboo are "cold arrow" and "walking stick."

SIDE ORDERS

Although up to 99 percent of the food they eat is bamboo, giant pandas actually are omnivores, which means that they eat both plants and meat. Besides eating roots, leaves, and flowers, such as crocuses and irises, they also eat small animals, such as rats, pikas, and fish.

DID YOU KNOW?

Giant pandas do not sleep at night — they sleep whenever they feel like it! Day and night, a giant panda wanders around its territory, looking for food. It will stop to sleep whenever and wherever it wants. Sometimes, the panda will sleep for a few hours, and, sometimes, for only a few minutes.

Danger!

No wild animals try to hunt healthy adult giant pandas. Only young pandas risk being attacked by predators. People are the giant panda's only real enemies. People cut down bamboo forests to use the wood and to make room for more houses and farms. They destroy so much of the forests that pandas are left without enough space to roam freely and without enough bamboo to eat.

Flowering Famine

Every fifty to one hundred years, an entire species of bamboo blooms, then drops its seeds and dies. The seeds sprout, but the new bamboo plants have to grow for six or seven years before they provide food for pandas. Losing such an important food supply means that many giant pandas may die.

No Hunting Allowed

In China, hunting giant pandas is against the law, and hunters may be punished by death. Even though hunting is not allowed, however, giant pandas are still in danger. Young pandas are captured and sent to zoos. Adult giant pandas are poached, or hunted illegally, for their fur coats, which are called pelts. One giant panda pelt can sell for as much as $100,000 on the **black market**. One reason people will pay so much for panda pelts is that they believe these pelts keep away ghosts or can help in predicting the future. For a large amount of money, some people are willing to hunt pandas illegally.

DANGEROUS SPOTS

Newborn pandas are small and easy to attack. If its mother is not nearby, a panda cub can become a quick meal for a predator such as the snow leopard. Like the giant panda, the snow leopard, which is also called an ounce, is a rare, endangered animal that lives high in the mountains of central Asia. A snow leopard has a beautiful, brownish gray coat with black spots on it.

A Panda's Day

 6:00 AM The sun was coming up. Giant pandas are mostly **nocturnal**, but many other animals are just waking when the sun comes up. The birds were especially noisy this morning.

 8:00 AM I like it when the sun comes up. Sunlight makes the air warmer. I set off with my cub in search of a morning feast.

 10:00 AM I found a great patch of my favorite kind of bamboo. It looks just like lots of walking sticks. My cub will be able to eat bamboo soon, so I showed him how to find the tastiest shoots.

 12:00 NOON After our meal, we sat down, camouflaged in the bamboo, and slept for a few hours. We cannot see very much in the daytime, anyway, because we have special eyes for seeing in the dark.

 3:00 PM I was very thirsty when I woke up. We were close to a stream, so we didn't have to go far to find a refreshing drink of water. Then, we spent a few more hours dozing.

 7:00 PM The sun was starting to set, but I was wide awake! I thought I heard a leopard so my cub and I climbed a tree to hide. When the leopard went away, we climbed back down.

9:00 PM We heard some loud rustling and hid behind a few trees. Some people walked by. We often see people. They never harm us, but you can't be too careful.

 12:00 MIDNIGHT We wandered into another panda's territory by mistake. Luckily, the panda had marked some trees with its scent to warn us, so we could avoid running into each other.

 2:00 AM I found some flowers to eat. They were good but not as tasty as bamboo. My cub was practicing climbing and crawling. He bumped himself a little when he fell off my shoulder.

 4:30 AM I found rats in my bamboo! If I had been able to catch one, I would have had a nice treat. I'm not a very good hunter, so the rats escaped. Maybe I'll have better luck next time.

 5:30 AM I would like to take a nap, but I'm not quite full, yet, and I have lots of food around me. I think I'll nibble a while longer.

Bear Cousins

Zoologists, who are scientists who study animals, do not agree on whether giant pandas belong to the bear family or the raccoon family. For many years, most zoologists grouped giant pandas with red pandas and raccoons. Today, more zoologists think giant pandas should be grouped with bears.

Big Brother

Giant pandas look a lot more like bears than like raccoons. Giant pandas and brown bears, the most common kind of bears, both have large heads and big bodies. Like a giant panda, a brown bear is an omnivore and, except when mating or when a mother is raising her cubs, it lives alone.

ICE GIANT

The polar bear is the biggest of all bears. This sleek, powerful animal is a great swimmer, and it can travel very far in freezing cold water. Unlike most other kinds of bears, polar bears eat a lot of meat.

BEAR TO BEAR

The polar bear is the largest bear. It can grow to be 10 feet (3 m) long.

The kodiak bear is like the grizzly bear, but bigger!

The grizzly bear may be the most **aggressive** kind of bear.

A giant panda is only half the size of a polar bear.

IT'S A BEAR

Scientific tests show that a giant panda's blood is more like the blood of a bear than like the blood of a red panda. A giant panda also has the same heavy body and short tail as a bear, but some of its bear cousins are so huge they make a giant panda look small.

Raccoon Relatives

A giant panda's closest relative may be the red panda, which is also called the lesser panda. They share many features, but not all zoologists agree on how the two pandas are related. The giant panda looks like a bear, while the red panda looks more like a raccoon. Like giant pandas, however, red pandas eat a lot of bamboo, and both kinds of pandas have the special "panda's thumb" on their front paws, which helps them grip the bamboo. Giant pandas and red pandas also have skull, tooth, and foot **structures** that are a lot alike, but different from both bears and raccoons.

Red Panda

The red panda is a nocturnal animal. It spends its days curled up on a branch, with its long, bushy tail covering its head or with its head tucked against its chest. At night, the red panda goes looking for food. It eats bamboo shoots, roots, fruit, and even small animals.

PLEISTOCENE PANDAS

Giant pandas have been around for thousands of years. In fact, their ancestors can be traced back to the Pleistocene Age, about two million years ago. Today, giant pandas live only in China, but they used to be far more widespread. At one time, they lived in other Asian countries, such as Burma and Vietnam, as well as in more of China. Changes in **climate**, the growth of towns and cities, and the shortage of bamboo forests have forced pandas to live in a very limited area.

RING-TAILED RACCOON

A raccoon is easy to recognize by its long, bushy, ringed tail and the band of dark fur that looks like a mask across its eyes. Raccoons live on the ground, up in a tree, or even in water. They eat fish, fruit, insects, lizards, and eggs.

HUMANS AND PANDAS

Giant pandas were a well-kept Chinese secret until the late 1860s, when a French missionary, named Père David, sent a panda pelt and skeleton back to Europe from China. It was not until the 1930s that people outside of Asia saw live pandas for the first time. The Chinese knew the giant panda was an unusual animal, and for hundreds of years, they treated it like a god. Today, the giant panda is a symbol for China in the same way that the bald eagle is a symbol for the United States. While some people are still hunting giant pandas, many other people are trying to save them and the bamboo forests in which they live.

PANDAS IN RESERVE

Giant pandas are an endangered species. In China, land is set aside for pandas in **reserves**, such as the Wolong Reserve, where hunting is not allowed and the bamboo forests cannot be destroyed. A giant panda is the well-known symbol of the World Wildlife Fund (WWF), which is an organization that works to protect rare animals.

DID YOU KNOW?

- In China, the government has officially named the giant panda a national treasure.

- The Chinese government has made several special gifts of pandas to other countries as symbols of its friendship.

- Giant pandas can be seen in every part of China, but only in drawings and paintings or as decorations and toys.

- Millions of children have owned toy pandas. A roly-poly black-and-white panda always looks cute and cuddly.

BEHIND BARS

Giant pandas are rare, so very few zoos have one. The dealer who bought the London Zoo's famous Chi-Chi from China had to trade three giraffes, two rhinos, two hippos, and two zebras to get her!

Glossary

AGGRESSIVE
Bold and forceful, usually the first to attack or start a fight.

ALTITUDES
Measurements of height, especially how high something is above Earth's surface or above the level of the sea.

BLACK MARKET
The business of buying and selling items that are against the law to buy or sell or that are under government control.

CAMOUFLAGE
A color, pattern, or appearance that helps an animal blend in with its surroundings.

CLIMATE
The normal type of weather in a particular area.

DIGEST
To break down food inside the body so its nutrients can be absorbed into the blood and used by the body.

DIGIT
A finger or a toe.

HERMITS
People who live alone and always try to stay away from others.

MAMMAL
A warm-blooded animal that has a backbone and hair or fur on its skin and that feeds its young with milk from the mother's body.

MOLARS
The flat, wide teeth at the back of the mouth that are used for grinding up or mashing hard or chewy foods.

NOCTURNAL
Most active at night and usually resting during the day.

NUTRIENTS
The parts of foods that keep animals strong and healthy.

PREDATORS
Animals that kill other animals for food.

RACCOONS
Small, meat-eating, North American mammals that have bushy, ringed tails and dark fur stretching across their eyes like a mask.

RESERVES
Areas of protected land where wild animals and plants can live in their natural habitats without being disturbed or harmed.

SPECIES
Groups of animals in which members of a group have many of the same physical features and behaviors and can mate with each other to produce offspring.

STRUCTURES
Arrangements of individual parts into a single unit.

TERRITORY
A large area of land claimed by someone or something for a particular use.

INDEX